Quotes for the Soul

Quotes & Self Analysis to Inspire Your Daily Life

Josh Folds

Souls of Influence

PALM CITY, FL

Quotes for th Soul/ Josh Folds
ISBN 978-0-578-57529-2

Dedication

I would like to dedicate this book to my family who made this possible. Mom and Dad thanks for always having my back and being great examples to follow. Tyler, London, Damon and Jordan you all drive me to be the very best I can be every day. The sky is the limit for all of you thanks for believing in me.

To my beautiful wife De Anna thanks for going through this crazy adventure called life side by side with me. You are my rock and I love you more than words will ever express. Thank you for always pushing me outside of my comfort zone to reach places I never thought I could. To all of my friends and colleagues over the years thanks for bringing out the best in me I hope this book can inspire you to find your greatness!

Finally to my Lord and Savior Jesus Christ I am eternally grateful for the endless blessings you have bestowed upon me. May this gift be a blessing to others to aid them along their journey.

*Just as a note: For any post on social media, please use #QuotesForTheSoul

Contents

January

January 1

Happy New Year! Now what?

"Do not let repetition fool you
into being ordinary"

———

Questions for the day

What will truly be different this year?

_____

_____

How can I hold myself accountable to the goals I set this year?

_____

_____

Choose to be great and make it a creative positive day!

January 2

"I can no longer be the version of my old self it is up to me to create my own unique identity"

Questions for the day

What is your brand and how would you define it to someone?

_____

_____

What steps will you take today to grow your brand?

_____

_____

Choose to be great and make it a creative positive day!

January 3

*"Anyone can be a manager but very few can lead
and lead with purpose"*

Questions for the day

Are you clear on your purpose personally and professionally?

_____

_____

Even if you do not have the title you want now what is
stopping you from being a leader to those around you?

_____

_____

Choose to be great and make it a creative positive day!

January 4

"Being vulnerable is just scratching the surface of becoming great"

———

Questions for the day

How can you become more vulnerable to stretch and grow your career?

_____

_____

What is the root cause as to what may be holding you back from growing?

_____

_____

Choose to be great and have a creative positive day!

January 5

"Others will check your social media feed just to see if you have failed"

———

Questions for the day

How will you minimize the noise around you to stay focused on your goals?

_____

_____

What are some things you can do to avoid unnecessary distractions around you?

_____

_____

Choose to be great and have a creative positive day!

January 6

*"Although losing causes temporary frustration,
hope is found in future opportunities"*

———

Questions for the day

What can you do to be better prepared for your next opportunity?

_____

_____

Do you have the tools and resources you need to win?

_____

_____

Choose to be great and have a creative positive day!

January 7

"Engagement creates outcomes so make sure you are the one leading the charge"

———

Questions for the day

What is holding you back from inspiring those around you?

_____

_____

Do others see you as a leader or just a peer?

_____

_____

Choose to be great and have a creative positive day!

January 8

"Time is just an excuse for lack of action"

———

Questions for the day

What needs to be on your calendar that is not there today?

_____

_____

What sacrifices are you willing to make to achieve your goals?

_____

_____

Choose to be great and have a creative positive day!

January 9

"Motivation should be the constant that drives results"

———

Questions for the day

What motivates you?

_____

_____

What changes can you make to set aside time to simply think
and be strategic about your personal growth?

_____

_____

Choose to be great and have a creative positive day!

January 10

"Do not wait for others to give you instructions rather take the lead and let them be the ones that ultimately follow your lead"

Questions for the day

Are you a leader or a follower?

_____

_____

What actions can you do today to improve your leadership skills?

_____

_____

Choose to be great and have a creative positive day!

January 11

"Your brand should be a reflection of your character"

———

Questions for the day

Does your brand truly reflect YOU?

_____

_____

What are some ways you can continue to drive and build your brand?

_____

_____

Choose to be great and have a creative positive day!

January 12

"Be the latest and greatest version of you"

Questions for the day

Are you growing or stuck in neutral?

_____

_____

Are you clear on the areas you need to continue to grow?

_____

_____

Choose to be great and have a creative positive day!

January 13

"Be willing to sacrifice bad habits or you will succumb to mediocrity"

Questions for the day

What are the bad habits you need to start shedding starting today?

_____

_____

What are the new habits you need to implement for success?

_____

_____

Choose to be great and have a creative positive day!

January 14

"Your life is not solely defined by your career you were made for more than just your job"

Questions for the day

What are some community activities you can support and give back your time to?

_____

_____

Are you contributing in your professional and personal life or does one dominate the other?

_____

_____

Choose to be great and have a creative positive day!

January 15

"Like a clock your dreams should never stop moving forward"

Questions for the day

Are you making progress on your goals?

_____

_____

What is holding you back from moving forward?

_____

_____

Choose to be great and have a creative positive day!

January 16

"Stop scrolling through your social media feed and get up and act upon your goals"

———

Questions for the day

Why do you have the urge to constantly check your social media?

_____

_____

Can you set aside time to do that so it does not consume a majority of your time?

_____

_____

Choose to be great and have a creative positive day!

January 17

"Consistency is the result of sustained intensity"

———

Questions for the day

What are the areas you lack consistency?

_____

_____

What are some things you can start doing today and drive more consistency in your personal and professional life?

_____

_____

Choose to be great and have a creative positive day!

January 18

"Laziness is the deterrent to success"

———

Questions for the day

What can you do to be more proactive versus reactive in your daily grind?

_____

_____

What truly motivates you to be great?

_____

_____

Choose to be great and have a creative positive day!

January 19

"At some point time will give up on your dreams"

———

Questions for the day

How are you benchmarking your progress?

_____

_____

What timelines do you have in place to reach your goals?

_____

_____

Choose to be great and have a creative positive day!

January 20

"Regret is the enemy of fulfillment"

Questions for the day

What is your biggest regret?

_____

_____

What can you do now to prevent future regret?

_____

_____

Choose to be great and have a creative positive day!

January 21

"Your character will either grow or deplete your fan base"

Questions for the day

What 3 words describe you?

_____

_____

What are you doing to build your base of advocates around you?

_____

_____

Choose to be great and have a creative positive day!

January 22

"Lack of organization is a symptom to the disease called failure"

———

Questions for the day

What is your defined process for success?

_____

_____

What are some things you need to get in order asap to prevent failure?

_____

_____

Choose to be great and have a creative positive day!

January 23

"Choose your surroundings wisely haters are waiting to bring you down"

———

Questions for the day

How many people can you truly call a friend?

_____

_____

Would your surroundings reflect those that can help you get to where you want to be?

_____

_____

Choose to be great and have a creative positive day!

January 24

"You are writing your own story without even knowing how it ends"

Questions for the day

What would this current chapter in your life be titled?

_____

_____

What is the legacy you want to leave behind?

_____

_____

Choose to be great and have a creative positive day!

January 25

"Today is the day I double down on myself and let others know around me the direction I am headed"

Questions for the day

Who have you enlisted to help you achieve your goals?

_____

_____

Are you all clear on where you are trying to go and how to get there?

_____

_____

Choose to be great and have a creative positive day!

January 26

"No one can tell you anything about your success you are the author of your own story"

———

Questions for the day

How can you minimize distractions around you to work further towards your goals?

_____

_____

If you have been knocked down what is stopping you from getting back up and reaching even higher?

_____

_____

Choose to be great and have a creative positive day!

January 27

"Your greatness is defined by your fulfillment inside of you"

Questions for the day

Are you satisfied with where you are at in life?

_____

_____

Depending on that answer what is it going to take to fill the void of fulfillment?

_____

_____

Choose to be great and have a creative positive day!

January 28

"Ideas usually sound good in theory but rarely get put into action"

Questions for the day

Where are the areas you know you could be making more of an impact but aren't putting forth the effort?

_____

_____

What are some things you can take action on today that will make a difference tomorrow?

_____

_____

Choose to be great and have a creative positive day!

January 29

"You have a gift that may not even be opened yet"

Questions for the day

Are you clear on the gift of you and the value you provide?

_____

_____

How can you share that gift more with others?

_____

_____

Choose to be great and have a creative positive day!

January 30

"Your candor is your best defense that can beat any offense"

Questions for the day

Are you telling people what they want to hear or what they need to hear?

_____

_____

How can you get more comfortable in tactfully speaking your mind to others?

_____

_____

Choose to be great and have a creative positive day!

January 31

"Create the environment that causes those around you to be inspired"

Questions for the day

Who is that one person around you that needs to be lifted up?

_____

_____

How do you get inspired and think how does that resonate with others?

_____

_____

Choose to be great and have a creative positive day!

February

February 1

"Discipline determines direction"

Questions for the day

Do you have the necessary routines in place to drive consistent success?

_____

_____

What are you doing to ensure you stay on track with your aspirations?

_____

_____

Choose to be great and have a creative positive day!

February 2

"Destiny is the belief that your hard work will take you to the destination you have dreamed of reaching"

Questions for the day

What are you destined to do?

_____

_____

Do you have a picture in mind of what that destiny fulfilled looks like?

_____

_____

Choose to be great and have a creative positive day!

February 3

"That feeling you woke up with this morning will determine the flow of your day"

———

Questions for the day

Do you have a routine in how you start your day?

_____

_____

What motivates you to get out of bed and be productive?

_____

_____

Choose to be great and have a creative positive day!

February 4

*"Stop worrying about those things out of your control
and focus on why you are the best at what you do"*

———

Questions for the day

What is in your control that you need to focus more on to reach
the next step from where you are now?

_____

_____

What are things you can be doing now to make that next step?

_____

_____

Choose to be great and have a creative positive day!

February 5

"Make those around you join your fan base by displaying consistency in your actions"

Questions for the day

Do others want to emulate your success?

_____

_____

What is one word others would use to describe you?

_____

_____

Choose to be great and have a creative positive day!

February 6

"You only get one shot at life there are no do overs so why can't today be the day you breakthrough whatever is holding you back from greatness!"

Questions for the day

What area in your life needs a breakthrough to move forward?

_____

_____

What is the one regret you have about your life and what steps can you take to prevent future regrets?

_____

_____

Choose to be great and have a creative positive day!

February 7

"No one can push you except for you so stop procrastinating and push forward"

———

Questions for the day

Where in your life do you feel stuck?

_____

_____

What are some actions you can take today to move forward?

_____

_____

Choose to be great and have a creative positive day!

February 8

"The future cannot happen without first taking care of the present"

———

Questions for today

Do you live in the world of what if?

_____

_____

Are you worried about your future personally or professionally?

_____

_____

What specifically are you worried about?

_____

_____

Choose to be great and have a creative positive day!

February 9

"A new day is here determine now how you will impact those around you"

Questions for the day

What is one thing you can do today to add value to someone around you?

_____

_____

What is one area you need to focus in on for your own wellbeing?

_____

_____

Choose to be great and have a creative positive day!

February 10

"You are a unique creation that is unlike anyone else around you so stop comparing and start caring"

Questions for the day

What can you do to show more care for those around you?

_____

_____

If you are comparing your life to someone else why?

_____

_____

Choose to be great and have a creative positive day!

February 11

"You can get unstuck at any time the choice is yours"

Questions for the day

What area do you feel stuck in?

_____

_____

What are some actions you can take today to get back on track and get unstuck?

_____

_____

Choose to be great and have a creative positive day!

February 12

"Life was not meant for you to wander in the dark instead see the light and seize your moment"

Questions for the day

What is your darkest moment personally or professionally?

_____

_____

What was your proudest moment?

_____

_____

How have these areas shaped your character of who you are today?

_____

_____

Choose to be great and have a creative positive day!

46

February 13

"You are the sum of your decisions yet at times you do not even know the formula for your own success"

Questions for the day

What are some decisions that you have made in the last 30 days that you are proud of?

_____

_____

Do you feel like you have the right recipe for success?

_____

_____

Choose to be great and have a creative positive day!

February 14

"True love comes from that which makes you feel the most fulfilled"

————

Questions for the day

Where do you find your fulfillment in life?

_____

_____

Are you truly fulfilled? If not what will do the trick?

_____

_____

Choose to be great and have a creative positive day!

February 15

"Work does not define you the person you are looking at in the morning while getting ready for work does"

———

Questions for the day

Are you proud of the person you have become?

_____

_____

When you look in the mirror what do you see?

_____

_____

Choose to be great and have a creative positive day!

February 16

"Surround yourself with those wanting you to succeed as the common path is filled with more haters than followers"

———

Questions for the day

Is the company that you keep the supporting kind that build you up or break you down?

_____

_____

Do those around you really have your best interest?

_____

_____

Choose to be great and have a creative positive day!

February 17

"Time is not going to slow down so why should you"

———

Questions for the day

Do you feel organized?

_____

_____

What are some things you do in order to make the most out of each day?

_____

_____

Choose to be great and have a creative positive day!

February 18

"The lifestyle you live will determine the work ethic you have"

Questions for the day

Are you happy with your current lifestyle?

_____

_____

What are some things that drive your work ethic?

_____

_____

Choose to be great and have a creative positive day!

February 19

"You are the only one who truly knows the effort needed for success"

———

Questions for the day

What is 1 area you know you need to focus in on to grow your career?

_____

_____

What are steps you can take today to challenge and grow your skills?

_____

_____

Choose to be great and have a creative positive day!

February 20

"Today is the day for you to speak your mind and say the inner feelings that need to be said"

———

Questions for the day

Who is someone you need to communicate with today to clear the air or advance a stale conversation?

_____

_____

What keeps you from expressing your true inner feelings?

_____

_____

Choose to be great and have a creative positive day!

February 21

"If your dreams do not cause anxiety you may need to rethink what you are dreaming about"

Questions for the day

Do you have anxiety? If so over what?

_____

_____

What are some ways you deal with anxiety?

_____

_____

Choose to be great and have a creative positive day!

February 22

"Tools and resources are only as good as the person using the toolkit"

Questions for the day

What more do you need in order to be more effective in your personal and professional life?

_____

_____

What more can you be doing to take advantage of the tools in front of you?

_____

_____

Choose to be great and have a creative positive day!

February 23

"Your state of mind will either be state of the art or a project in process"

Questions for the day

What are some current gaps in your professional life?

_____

_____

What are the areas you can work on today to help close those gaps?

_____

_____

Choose to be great and have a creative positive day!

February 24

"Your race to be perfect is losing to those who run with consistency"

———

Questions for the day

Are you trying to keep up with those around you?

_____

_____

Are the things you are doing sustainable and filled with consistent behaviors?

_____

_____

Choose to be great and have a creative positive day!

February 25

"Your exhaustion is caused by your own misuse of energy"

———

Questions for the day

What areas of your life are you stressing over?

_____

_____

What are some things you could do today to put yourself more at ease while focusing on the task at hand?

_____

_____

Choose to be great and have a creative positive day!

February 26

"You are the channel to your own success"

Questions for the day

If you had to describe yourself as a tv channel what channel would it be and why?

_____

_____

What are some ways you can ensure you are feeding your brain the right energy needed for success?

_____

_____

Choose to be great and have a creative positive day!

February 27

"Create the culture that will be here long after you are gone"

———

Questions for the day

How would you define your current work environment?

_____

_____

What are some things you can do to drive the culture in your current company?

_____

_____

Choose to be great and have a creative positive day!

February 28

*"Get out of the passenger seat and take your rightful spot as
the driver of your own destiny"*

Questions for the day

What are some areas in your life that have taken a backseat and
are screaming for your attention?

_____

_____

What can you do today to get back on track?

_____

_____

Choose to be great and have a creative positive day!

February 29

"A leap of faith can never be a deterrent for your success"

Questions for the day

What is an area you would like to go out on a limb on and take a chance on yourself?

_____

_____

What is keeping you from taking that leap?

_____

_____

Choose to be great and have a creative positive day!

March

March 1

"New month new you start off with the right pursuit"

Questions for the day

What are some things you are currently pursuing?

_____

_____

Do those areas fall in line with your personal and professional goals?

_____

_____

Choose to be great and have a creative positive day!

March 2

"Determination will ease the frustration on your pathway to success"

Questions for the day

What is 1 area you would say you are most determined to succeed at right now?

_____

_____

How does that focus align with your goals?

_____

_____

Choose to be great and have a creative positive day!

March 3

"Money may provide temporary happiness but your health provides long term enjoyment"

———

Questions for the day

What do you do to focus on your health?

_____

_____

What are some steps you can take today to ensure a healthy lifestyle?

_____

_____

Choose to be great and have a creative positive day!

March 4

"You control the remote to your life so do not get stuck watching the same channel"

———

Questions for the day

Is your daily routine a repeat episode?

_____

_____

What can you do today to break up any unhealthy routines you may have?

_____

_____

Choose to be great and have a creative positive day!

March 5

"Today is the day that I refuse to be held captive by the nonstop thoughts and emotions that consume my energy"

Questions for the day

What are some thoughts going through your mind as you start your day?

_____

_____

What are some things you can do to remain calm and positive throughout the day?

_____

_____

Choose to be great and have a creative positive day!

March 6

"Your legacy is only as good as the impressions you want left behind wherever you go"

———

Questions for the day

What do you want your legacy to be?

_____

What is the impression you make on others?

_____

Are you happy with your responses to the first 2 questions?

_____

If not what can you do to change?

_____

Choose to be great and have a creative positive day!

March 7

"Your character is the way you treat those around you when you genuinely are not looking to get anything back in return"

Questions for the day

What type of character would those around you say you have?

_____

_____

Are you proud of the person you have become?

_____

_____

If you could change 1 thing about yourself what would it be?

_____

_____

Choose to be great and have a creative positive day!

March 8

"Fear is the emotion that can cancel out all progress"

———

Questions for the day

What keeps you up at night?

_____

_____

What is your biggest concern personally and professionally?

_____

_____

How do you overcome your fears?

_____

_____

Choose to be great and have a creative positive day!

March 9

"The sibling to wasted talent is mediocrity"

Questions for the day

Why do you think most people just simply accept their current situation?

_____

_____

Why are you different?

_____

_____

Choose to be great and have a creative positive day!

March 10

*"Believe to your core that you were meant for so much more
and watch your stock rise"*

———

Questions for the day

What is your biggest strength and what can you do to showcase
that strength more?

_____

_____

What are some other areas you would like to improve on from a
professional standpoint?

_____

_____

Choose to be great and have a creative positive day!

March 11

"In life we need to all continue to be students and expand our intellectual minds"

———

Questions for the day

What are some areas you would like to learn more about with your current career?

_____

_____

What is keeping you from pushing your career further at a faster pace?

_____

_____

Choose to be great and have a creative positive day!

March 12

"Be grateful for those around you that truly want you to succeed"

Questions for the day

Do you take out enough time to recognize those around you?

_____

_____

Do you spend time saying thank you to your employees no matter what level they are at?

_____

_____

Choose to be great and have a creative positive day!

March 13

"The success bar can only go as high as you can raise it"

Questions for the day

Are your expectations in line for what you truly want to achieve?

_____

_____

What else can you be doing today to get the exposure necessary for future growth?

_____

_____

Choose to be great and have a creative positive day!

March 14

"Your body language can inspire or disengage your audience"

Questions for the day

What does your body language say about your attitude?

_____

_____

What can you do differently today to ensure proper perception about your engagement going forward?

_____

_____

Choose to be great and have a creative positive day!

March 15

"There is no one to blame for your lack of success except YOU"

———

Questions for the day

What are things you can be doing today to cause a greater outcome?

_____

_____

Choose to be great and have a creative positive day!

March 16

"Patience is what is needed to craft and hire the perfect candidate"

Questions for the day

What areas do you feel pressured?

_____

_____

How does your profile appear externally?

_____

_____

Choose to be great and have a creative positive day!

March 17

"Confidence will carry your career"

———

Questions for the day

What more can you be doing to spend time with someone that needs you to help develop them?

_____

_____

What is the source of your confidence?

_____

_____

Choose to be great and have a creative positive day!

March 18

"Those who procrastinate are usually those that take up the most amount of your time"

Questions for the day

How would you characterize your ability to hustle?

_____

_____

What is 1 area you can commit to doing a better job in overall?

_____

_____

Choose to be great and have a creative positive day!

March 19

"The only hazard in the road is the hazard between the radio and your brain"

———

Questions for the day

What are the thoughts that are in your mind daily?

_____

_____

What can you be doing to become more productive?

_____

_____

Choose to be great and have a creative positive day!

March 20

"The way you communicate speaks volumes to your productivity"

Questions for the day

How is the tone in the place you work?

_____

_____

How much support do you get for the task on hand?

_____

_____

Choose to be great and have a creative positive day!

March 21

"Anxiety can bring down the bridges we have built to sustain"

———

Questions for the day

What makes you anxious?

_____

_____

What is the biggest bridge you have ever faced and how did you overcome it?

_____

_____

Choose to be great and have a creative positive day!

March 22

"Your talent will only take you so far it is your inner core that will take you to the next level"

Questions for the day

What is your next step and what are you doing to ensure you take it?

_____

_____

Choose to be great and have a creative positive day!

March 23

"Your journey has only begun and only you will be able to fill out the rest of the pages"

———

Questions for the day

What did you want to be when you were growing up?

_____

_____

Are you happy with how things have worked out for you thus far?

_____

_____

Choose to be great and have a creative positive day!

March 24

"Another quarter may come to an end but your daily grind must continue to rise above the rest"

———

Questions for the day

How often do you reflect on your performance?

———————————————————

———————————————————

What specifically do you review?

———————————————————

———————————————————

Choose to be great and have a creative positive day!

March 25

"The only true safety feature you need is having a GPS that leads to your success"

———

Questions for the day

Which direction are you headed in your current review of your career?

_____

_____

What else is needed along the way for you to be the most effective person at work and at home?

_____

_____

Choose to be great and have a creative positive day!

March 26

"Be the difference to stir the pot when necessary"

Questions for the day

Do you get true honest responses to hard hitting questions?

_____

_____

What is some recent feedback you have received from someone who has worked for you?

_____

_____

Choose to be great and have a creative positive day!

March 27

"Time is the necessary evil that creates dysfunction"

Questions for the day

What type of dysfunction are you currently facing?

_____

_____

How does time play a factor in your decision making?

_____

_____

Choose to be great and have a creative positive day!

March 28

"Be bold be relevant be candid be YOU"

Questions for the day

Do you bring your full self to work?

_____

_____

What can you do to stand out from the rest?

_____

_____

Choose to be great and have a creative positive day!

March 29

"Intensity is the brother of consistency "

Questions for you

What level of intensity do you show outwardly and towards what?

_____

_____

How can you become more consistent in your behaviors?

_____

_____

Choose to be great and have a creative positive day!

March 30

"Candor could lead to change which could be a positive or a negative the choice is yours"

Questions for the day

Do you display candor when in meetings?

_____

_____

Can you take it when others are candid to you in their feedback?

_____

_____

Choose to be great and have a creative positive day!

March 31

"The end of a month signals a beginning of another chapter"

Questions for the day

What are some areas you grew in during the first quarter of the year?

_____

_____

What is your focus for the 2nd quarter?

_____

_____

Choose to be great and have a creative positive day!

April

April 1

"The only fool is the one who doesn't pursue greatness"

———

Questions for the day

What do you believe is your true calling in life?

_____

_____

What is getting in the way from you pursuing your true desires?

_____

_____

Choose to be great and have a creative positive day!

April 2

"What is out of your control should be out of your mind"

Questions for the day

What are those things you truly need to release from your thoughts?

_____

_____

What are some steps you can take starting today to be more present?

_____

_____

Choose to be great and have a creative positive day!

April 3

"Change should be the fuel that drives your engine of success"

Questions for the day

What are some things you need to do to cause positive change in your life?

_____

_____

Do you have the energy to focus on this area?

_____

_____

Choose to be great and have a creative positive day!

April 4

"Your future can't be lived until your focus is on the present"

———

Questions for the day

What are some things you can be doing to focus more on the task in front of you?

_____

_____

Do you feel like you are organized?

_____

_____

Choose to be great and have a creative positive day!

April 5

"Your talent can only take you so far you must execute consistently to maximize your return"

––––––––

Questions for the day

Do you feel like you are consistent with the right behaviors to drive success?

_____

_____

Do you feel like you are achieving the goals you set out for yourself to start the year?

_____

_____

Choose to be great and have a creative positive day!

April 6

"They say the best defense is an explosive offense well then why are you always stuck on defense?"

Questions for the day

What can you do today to be more proactive in your overall productivity?

_____

_____

Are you truly moving forward in your career?

_____

_____

Choose to be great and have a creative positive day!

April 7

"Your attitude will define your longitude"

Questions for the day

What needs to change in your attitude to be more consistent with how you impact those around you?

_____

_____

How do you feel you are perceived by others?

_____

_____

Choose to be great and have a creative positive day!

April 8

"Your mind can truly defeat your soul you must cleanse yourself of negativity"

Questions for the day

What are you feeding your mind and how does that impact your daily productivity?

_____

_____

In your down time how are you using it for YOU?

_____

_____

Choose to be great and have a creative positive day!

April 9

"You are the one constant that can impact someone today do not waste the opportunity"

Questions for the day

Who is that one person you know needs someone to talk to?

_____

_____

What is holding you back from mentoring someone?

_____

_____

Choose to be great and have a creative positive day!

April 10

"When the odds are stacked against you that is when you should be performing at your best"

Questions for the day

How do you handle adversity?

_____

_____

How do you handle stress personally and professionally?

_____

_____

Choose to be great and have a creative positive day!

April 11

"Today was not meant to be wasted so act with urgency and create the moment"

———

Questions for the day

What can you do in order to act more with a sense of urgency towards your aspirations?

_____

_____

How well do you feel you are managing your time?

_____

_____

Choose to be great and have a creative positive day!

April 12

*"The enrichment of your life is found through the eyes
of your soul"*

———

Questions for the day

Are you fulfilled?

_____

_____

What would you define as a life of fulfillment?

_____

_____

Choose to be great and have a creative positive day!

April 13

"Do not be dependent on others in fact learn to stand on your own and be a soul of influence"

Questions for the day

Who do you feel you are dependent on in order to function day to day?

_____

_____

Do you see yourself as an influencer?

_____

_____

Choose to be great and have a creative positive day!

April 14

"Do not be defined by a moment in time rather leave a legacy of greatness"

Questions for the day

What do you feel you are known for?

_____

_____

Do you feel there is a positive perception of your abilities from those around you?

_____

_____

Choose to be great and have a creative positive day!

April 15

"There is no need to feel taxed instead focus all of your efforts to buck the trend and break the norm"

———

Questions for the day

What are your goals for retirement?

_____

_____

What is missing from your life that needs to be implemented to achieve your goals?

_____

_____

Choose to be great and have a creative positive day!

April 16

"Keep in mind you are always on stage regardless if the lights are on or off"

Questions for the day

How do you ensure a true work life balance?

_____

_____

What boundaries do you set to ensure you have proper balance?

_____

_____

Choose to be great and have a creative positive day!

April 17

"What challenges you and tests you is ultimately what will develop you"

———

Questions for the day

Do you honestly feel challenged thus far this year in your role?

_____

_____

Are you receiving consistent feedback towards your development?

_____

_____

Choose to be great and have a creative positive day!

April 18

"You do not have to be in a leadership role to be an impactful coach to those around you"

Questions for the day

Do you view yourself as a coach to those around you?

_____

_____

Do you offer your assistance to help coach others?

_____

_____

Choose to be great and have a creative positive day!

April 19

"The way to your golden path is only in the direction you are currently headed"

—————

Questions for the day

Are you clear in the direction you are headed?

_____

_____

Who do you need to enlist on your journey to get where you are headed?

_____

_____

Choose to be great and have a creative positive day!

April 20

"Life is full of temporary happiness so do something that has a lasting impact"

———

Questions for the day

How can you make a lasting impact?

_____

_____

What more do you need to be more of an impact player?

_____

_____

Choose to be great and have a creative positive day!

April 21

"The input you give and get will only be as good as the output that is put into action"

Questions for the day

What are the daily habits you have in place to push ahead?

_____

_____

What changes need to be made to make more time for your own growth?

_____

_____

Choose to be great and have a creative positive day!

April 22

"The end result of all of your days will only be as good as the quality you delivered"

———

Questions for the days

What are the time wasters in your life?

_____

_____

What do you need to do to drive more quality outcomes on a daily basis?

_____

_____

Choose to be great and have a creative positive day!

April 23

"Your life was not meant to come and go in passing to just be a spectator"

Questions for the day

How do you feel right now about how you have lived your life?

_____

_____

Anything you would say to your younger self if you had the chance?

_____

_____

Choose to be great and have a creative positive day!

April 24

"Your thirst for more has made you come up empty on most occasions"

Questions for the day

What is it that you believe your heart truly desires?

_____

_____

Are your wants getting in the way of your true needs?

_____

_____

Choose to be great and have a creative positive day!

April 25

"True glory is found in the days leading up to you overcoming your own fears and truly winning"

Questions for the day

What are you most fearful of?

_____

_____

Does that fear impact your progress?

_____

_____

Choose to be great and have a creative positive day!

April 26

"The sounds in your head should be sounds of progress"

———

Questions for the day

What thoughts run through your mind on a consistent basis?

_____

_____

Are you doing anything to have more control over your thinking?

_____

_____

Choose to be great and have a creative positive day!

April 27

"Haters are common for those achieving on a consistent basis"

Questions for the day

How do you handle those against you?

_____

_____

What are some steps you take to channel out the negative noises around you?

_____

_____

Choose to be great and have a creative positive day!

April 28

"Focus on you more and reap the benefits"

Questions for the day

What do you need to do in order for more YOU time in your life?

_____

_____

What are your hobbies?

_____

_____

Choose to be great and have a creative positive day!

April 29

"True success is found in how you define it so do not settle for anyone else's definition"

Questions for the day

What is your definition of success?

_____

_____

How can you ensure progress towards your ultimate view of success?

_____

_____

Choose to be great and have a creative positive day!

April 30

"Your pace and progress will determine your place and process"

Questions for the day

What is your process towards personal development?

_____

_____

What is the end result you are seeking?

_____

_____

Choose to be great and have a creative positive day!

May

May 1

"Your aspirations have an expiration date do not let your dreams go stale"

Questions for the day

What are you doing to stay focused on your aspirations?

_____

_____

What can you do to be more consistent with your efforts to push forward towards your dreams?

_____

_____

Choose to be great and have a creative positive day!

May 2

"You can't be in full control of every detail in your life so let go and your character will prosper"

———

Questions for the day

What are some things you need to give up control on?

_____

_____

Do you feel you are a controlling person?

_____

_____

Choose to be great and have a creative positive day!

May 3

"Time will not wait for your procrastination"

Questions for the day

In what areas do you need to be more proactive?

_____

_____

What is keeping you from accomplishing more in your life?

_____

_____

Choose to be great and have a creative positive day!

May 4

*"Instead of having too much pride drop your guard
and be the guide"*

Questions for the day

Do you consider yourself a prideful person?

_____

_____

Are you a follower or a leader?

_____

_____

Choose to be great and have a creative positive day!

May 5

"Every day should be a celebration of progress"

———

Questions for the day

What motivates you to get of bed and start your day?

_____

_____

What do you do to celebrate progress in your life?

_____

_____

Choose to be great and have a creative positive day!

May 6

"Just when you think you have failed think again you are a work in progress and success is your destiny"

———

Questions for the day

What would you consider to be your biggest failure in life?

_____

_____

When you have a setback how do you handle it?

_____

_____

Choose to be great and have a creative positive day!

May 7

"A breakthrough is waiting for you just open your eyes, see the big picture and trust the process"

Questions for the day

What would a breakthrough be for you?

_____

_____

What is your big picture?

_____

_____

Choose to be great and have a creative positive day!

May 8

"Your beliefs will determine your basis for living"

Questions for the day

What are your personal beliefs?

_____

_____

What do you believe is your ultimate destination?

_____

_____

Choose to be great and have a creative positive day!

May 9

"Worry will not do a single bit of good to keep you headed in the right direction"

Questions for the day

What are some things you are worrying about today?

_____

_____

What would happen if you were to fully release your worries?

_____

_____

Choose to be great and have a creative positive day!

May 10

*"No quote or ounce of motivation can overcome
a negative attitude"*

———

Questions for the day

How do others perceive your attitude?

_____

_____

How do you handle negative people around you?

_____

_____

Choose to be great and have a creative positive day!

May 11

"Focus on every interaction and ensure you are making a positive impact"

———

Questions for the day

Who is that one person you know needs some attention today?

_____

_____

What more can you be doing to positively impact those around you?

_____

_____

Choose to be great and have a creative positive day!

May 12

"Your outlook on your life will determine the way you treat others around you"

Questions for the day

What do you feel your gift is?

_____

_____

What would others say your gift is?

_____

_____

Choose to be great and have a creative positive day!

May 13

"To truly elevate to the next level we must be transparent with our weaknesses"

Questions for the day

Do you consider yourself vulnerable?

_____

_____

What are some things you do to improve upon areas you feel weak?

_____

_____

Choose to be great and have a creative positive day!

May 14

"Your outlook on your life will determine the way you treat others around you"

Questions for the day

Do you ever pause and reflect on how you have been treating those around you?

_____

_____

What is your overall outlook on your life?

_____

_____

Choose to be great and have a creative positive day!

May 15

"There will never be a better time than now to make the changes necessary to live the life waiting for you"

Questions for the day

What changes do you need to make in order to feel like you are on the right track?

_____

_____

What is holding you back from making changes in your life?

_____

_____

Choose to be great and have a creative positive day!

May 16

"Your story is coming together day by day make it a good one"

———

Questions for the day

What chapter of your life are you currently in?

_____

_____

What chapters are you behind in writing?

_____

_____

Choose to be great and have a creative positive day!

May 17

"In a blink of an eye your circumstance can change thus why preparation is critical"

Questions for the day

Is your house in order?

_____

_____

What are some areas you need to be more organized?

_____

_____

Choose to be great and have a creative positive day!

May 18

"Truth be told you can make decisions today that can alter your current path"

Questions for the day

What are some decisions you are facing today?

_____

_____

How will these decisions impact the path you are on?

_____

_____

Choose to be great and have a creative positive day!

May 19

"You are the template for what hard work should look like"

Questions for the day

How would others view your work ethic?

_____

_____

What are some areas that you can improve your current life template?

_____

_____

Choose to be great and have a creative positive day!

May 20

"Humility will be the secret ingredient needed to lead others"

———

Questions for the day

If you are not in a leadership role now what can you still be doing to lead others?

_____

_____

Do you consider yourself a humble person?

_____

_____

Choose to be great and have a creative positive day!

May 21

"At our darkest moment we can find glory in the most uncommon places"

———

Questions for the day

Do you ever feel depressed?

_____

_____

If so what are you depressed about?

_____

_____

Choose to be great and have a creative positive day!

May 22

"Your faith is the fuel to get you to your eternal destiny"

Questions for the day

What do you have faith in?

_____

_____

What is your view on eternity?

_____

_____

Choose to be great and have a creative positive day!

May 23

"Possibly the one thing you may need to grow is the one area you have fear to face"

———

Questions for the day

What things do you do to get outside of your comfort zone?

_____

_____

What happens when you go outside of your comfort zone?

_____

_____

Choose to be great and have a creative positive day!

May 24

"The beauty of life is found through the eyes of your soul"

Questions for the day

What do you do to take time to enjoy the sights and sounds around you?

_____

_____

Are you spending enough quality time with friends and family?

_____

_____

Choose to be great and have a creative positive day!

May 25

"The more you learn the more you grow thus the more you impact others"

———

Questions for the day

What do you personally do to focus on your own development?

_____

_____

How do you use your experience and skills to impact others?

_____

_____

Choose to be great and have a creative positive day!

May 26

"A minor setback may be just what you need for a major comeback"

———

Questions for the day

What are some recent setbacks you have faced?

_____

_____

How have they shaped the person you are today?

_____

_____

Choose to be great and have a creative positive day!

May 27

"The energy you bring to every interaction is a reflection of your true nature"

Questions for the day

Are you mentally present for those interactions you have recently had?

_____

_____

Do you put others first before your own needs?

_____

_____

Choose to be great and have a creative positive day!

May 28

"The dates on a calendar are just a reminder of how far behind you are from your dreams"

———

Questions for the day

Do you have timelines to your goals?

_____

_____

What do you do when running past due?

_____

_____

Choose to be great and have a creative positive day!

May 29

"You truly can only graduate to the next stage of your life after you have left your past behind"

———

Questions for the day

What parts of your past keep you from living in the present?

_____

_____

What are some areas of your life that you need to move on from?

_____

_____

Choose to be great and have a creative positive day!

May 30

"A new day is a new sign that great things will come your way if you simply keep an open mind"

Questions for the day

What are some areas that you would say you have been close minded?

_____

_____

How can you keep a more open mind towards life?

_____

_____

Choose to be great and have a creative positive day!

May 31

"The end of the month marks a great time to have accountability directly related to your progress"

Questions for the day

5 months into the year how do you feel you are doing?

_____

_____

Do you have an accountability partner?

_____

_____

Choose to be great and have a creative positive day!

June

June 1

"While seasons may change one thing should remain constant and that is your will to win"

Questions for the day

How consistent are you with your will to win?

_____

_____

Would you say you have a strong work ethic?

_____

_____

Choose to be great and have a creative positive day!

June 2

"You cannot reclaim yesterday but you can define your tomorrow by your actions today"

———

Questions for the day

What are some things you can do today in order for you to be ahead of where you need to be tomorrow?

_____

_____

What gets in the way of you not accomplishing your daily tasks?

_____

_____

Choose to be great and have a creative positive day!

June 3

"Bitterness will not only leave a bad taste in your mouth but will leave you feeling defeated"

Questions for the day

Do you feel like you forgive others easily?

_____

_____

What is one thing you need to let go so you can move forward?

_____

_____

Choose to be great and have a creative positive day!

June 4

*"You are dying by the second so focus on every interaction
and
make every second count"*

───────

Questions for the day

How is your physical health?

_____

_____

Mental health?

_____

_____

Choose to be great and have a creative positive day!

June 5

"Emptiness may just be the feeling you need to light the fire of greatness inside of you"

———

Questions for the day

When you are at your lowest point what do you do to bounce back?

_____

_____

Do you feel like you have a fire lit inside of you to push forward in your life?

_____

_____

Choose to be great and have a creative positive day!

June 6

"Excuses are the symptoms leading to a dreadful disease of your mind and body"

Questions for the day

What excuses have you been making lately in your life and why?

_____

_____

What can you to in order to limit your excuses and excuses from others?

_____

_____

Choose to be great and have a creative positive day!

June 7

"Your fragrance for life should be the smell of progress"

———

Questions for the day

How is your environment at home and at work?

_____

_____

What can you do today to make a more positive impact to those around you?

_____

_____

Choose to be great and have a creative positive day!

June 8

"The consistency of winning can drive the consistency of internal and external growth"

Questions for the day

What are some areas you need more consistency?

_____

_____

What does winning in life look like to you?

_____

_____

Choose to be great and have a creative positive day!

June 9

To be great you must first be broken"

———

Questions for the day

Have you ever been completely broken?

_____

_____

What stops you from growing personally and professionally?

_____

_____

Choose to be great and have a creative positive day!

June 10

"The value of one's life can be determined by his or her reflection on what truly is important"

Questions for the day

How do you define your true value to others?

_____

_____

What are the top 3 most important things in your life?

_____

_____

Choose to be great and have a creative positive day!

June 11

"Your follow through should mirror your expectations of others"

Questions for the day

Do you consider yourself responsive to others?

_____

_____

What is your preferred method of communication and why?

_____

_____

Choose to be great and have a creative positive day!

June 12

"True fellowship with others is the essence of learning and growing"

Questions for the day

Do you have a large network or keep a small circle?

_____

_____

What are some conversations you need to have but have held off from having?

_____

_____

Choose to be great and have a creative positive day!

June 13

"Hard work pays off but only if you have paid your dues by working hard"

Questions for the day

What are some secrets to your success?

_____

_____

What is the hardest job you have ever had?

_____

_____

Choose to be great and have a creative positive day!

June 14

"Your personal brand should reflect your inner soul thus showing the real you"

———

Questions for the day

Do you feel that you are authentic?

_____

_____

Does the outer you reflect the inner you?

_____

_____

Choose to be great and have a creative positive day!

June 15

"You know who truly has your best interest in mind so do not waste time with those that do not"

Questions for the day

Do you feel like you have the right advocates around you?

_____

_____

Do you have others best interest in mind when interacting?

_____

_____

Choose to be great and have a creative positive day!

June 16

"Sometimes it is ok to hit the pause button and reflect in order to stay the course"

Questions for the day

What do you do in order to slow down and measure your pace and progress?

_____

_____

How do you feel about the pace your life is moving?

_____

_____

Choose to be great and have a creative positive day!

June 17

"Trust can only be given if it has truly been earned by action"

———

Questions for the day

How long does it take you to trust someone?

_____

_____

Is it easy for you to trust others?

_____

_____

Choose to be great and have a creative positive day!

June 18

"You will only go as high as your mind will allow"

Questions for the day

What is your overall vision for your future?

_____

_____

Do you feel like you limit yourself at times due to doubt and fear?

_____

_____

Choose to be great and have a creative positive day!

June 19

"To be great it starts with this very moment and then everything you do going forward"

Questions for the day

Have you unlocked your greatness?

_____

_____

Do you feel as if you take advantage of the free time you have to grow and move forward?

_____

_____

Choose to be great and have a creative positive day!

June 20

"Be ready for anything and always expect everything"

Questions for the day

Would you consider yourself someone who is prepared to face anything in life?

_____

_____

What more can you do in order to be more prepared for what life throws your way?

_____

_____

Choose to be great and have a creative positive day!

June 21

"Only you truly know what it is going to take to make things happen so take that next step and do it"

Questions for the day

Do you let things happen or make things happen?

_____

_____

What is holding you back from making a broader impact?

_____

_____

Choose to be great and have a creative positive day!

June 22

"Be humble in everything but confident with anything that comes your way"

———

Questions for the day

Do you consider yourself a humble person?

_____

_____

What are some areas of your life that could use more confidence?

_____

_____

Choose to be great and have a creative positive day!

June 23

"Your dose of motivation is only as good as your innovation"

Questions for the day

What do you do to innovate and create your own identity?

_____

_____

Are you truly motivated to do more?

_____

_____

Choose to be great and have a creative positive day!

June 24

"You are the author of your own story make sure what you write today is truly worth reading"

———

Questions for the day

Are you pleased with the life you have lived thus far?

_____

_____

What changes would you make?

_____

_____

Choose to be great and have a creative positive day!

June 25

"Do not let others pass by like the wind rather make the most of every interaction by being more present"

―――――

Questions for the day

When you have your personal time are you physically and mentally present?

_____

_____

Do you give others your full attention when conversing one on one?

_____

_____

Choose to be great and have a creative positive day!

June 26

"Today is your day do not let anyone rob you of what is meant to be"

———

Questions for the day

How well do you block out negativity from those around you?

_____

_____

What do you do to maintain consistent focus?

_____

_____

Choose to be great and have a creative positive day!

June 27

"True glory is found in your definition of living"

———

Questions for the day

What are you living for?

_____

_____

What does living your best life look like to you?

_____

_____

Choose to be great and have a creative positive day!

June 28

"Progress is measured by little wins that amount to big victories"

———

Questions for the day

What is an area that you need to pay more attention to and make further progress?

_____

_____

What are you doing to celebrate that little things that add up to make a bigger impact?

_____

_____

Choose to be great and have a creative positive day!

June 29

"Culture can be defined by the attitude from you and those around you"

———

Questions for the day

What type of tone do you try to set each day for you and those around you?

_____

_____

What is the best culture you have ever worked in and why?

_____

_____

Choose to be great and have a creative positive day!

June 30

"Candid feedback is the gateway to effective personal and professional growth"

Questions for the day

What are some areas you are currently being coached on?

_____

_____

Do you get consistent meaningful feedback?

_____

_____

Choose to be great and have a creative positive day!

July

July 1

"The start of the 3rd quarter reminds us of the adjustments that must be made before the game is over"

Questions for the day

What are the adjustments you need to make to stay the course?

_____

_____

What have you learned from the first half of this year that you can do better the 2nd half of the year?

_____

_____

Choose to be great and have a creative positive day!

July 2

"Be mindful not to let your talents rot away while chasing after a meaningless dream"

———

Questions for the day

Do you feel like you have the right goals aligned to the right behaviors?

_____

_____

Are your dreams aligned to reality?

_____

_____

Choose to be great and have a creative positive day!

July 3

"It is hard for others to appreciate your struggle if they only see your present not your past"

Questions for the day

What is the essence of your life story?

_____

_____

Anything you would do different if you had another chance?

_____

_____

Choose to be great and have a creative positive day!

July 4

"As we celebrate freedom we celebrate the humility we need in order to lead others to their definition of freedom"

Questions for the day

What is your definition of freedom?

_____

_____

Do others see arrogance or humility in your actions?

_____

_____

Choose to be great and have a creative positive day!

July 5

"Sometimes you need to be crushed so that you can be raised in greatness"

Questions for the day

What has your lowest point been in life?

_____

_____

What has been your greatest comeback?

_____

_____

Choose to be great and have a creative positive day!

July 6

"Just when you think it is ok to give up remember why you started your journey in the first place and push forward"

―――――

Questions for the day

How do you get rid of self-doubt and fear?

_____

_____

What are some things you do to push forward and stay on track?

_____

_____

Choose to be great and have a creative positive day!

July 7

"All the Sundays of your youth tell a story think about those you are impacting that are building their story"

———

Questions for the day

What do you do to give back to your community?

_____

_____

What do your Sundays look like?

_____

_____

Choose to be great and have a creative positive day!

July 8

"Purpose with a passion leads to progress towards a plan"

Questions for the day

Are you clear as to what your purpose is?

_____

_____

What is your true passion?

_____

_____

Choose to be great and have a creative positive day!

July 9

"Many succumb to the struggle while few realize true self-identity"

———

Questions for the day

How would you define your self-identity?

_____

_____

Does the perception from others reflect your own view of your identity?

_____

_____

Choose to be great and have a creative positive day!

July 10

"The more that is given to you the more likely it will never be enough"

Questions for the day

What drives you and motivates you?

_____

_____

How do you know when you are truly fulfilled?

_____

_____

Choose to be great and have a creative positive day!

July 11

*"The opportunity in front of you can only be as rewarding as
the journey you are about to embark upon"*

Questions for the day

Is what is next for you truly worth the next journey in your life?

_____

_____

How do you know when the right opportunity presents itself?

_____

_____

Choose to be great and have a creative positive day!

July 12

"Read and react to a point where you implement what you have read"

Questions for the day

What are some things you know you need to put into action?

_____

_____

What is the last book you have read?

_____

_____

Choose to be great and have a creative positive day!

July 13

"The battle within could just be the light to the fire needed to find victory"

———

Questions for the day

What is a recent victory you could share?

_____

_____

What is a recent battle you have gone through and how did you overcome it?

_____

_____

Choose to be great and have a creative positive day!

July 14

"Sometimes the bar is set so high that we fail to improve our reach and raise the bar to a new level"

———

Questions for the day

What is keeping you from pushing to that next level?

_____

_____

How can you be the bar and be the measurement of success in whatever you are striving to achieve?

_____

_____

Choose to be great and have a creative positive day!

July 15

"The start of something great starts the moment you get vulnerable and real about where you need to improve"

———

Questions for the day

Do you feel like you are vulnerable to those around you to provide meaningful feedback?

_____

_____

Do you encourage those around you to be vulnerable?

_____

_____

Choose to be great and have a creative positive day!

July 16

"Only you know what it will truly take to accomplish your destiny"

Questions for the day

What is running through your mind when you wake up and start your day?

_____

_____

What can you do in order to feed your mind positivity?

_____

_____

Choose to be great and have a creative positive day!

July 17

"Seek knowledge instead of gratification and you will gain courage to grow"

Questions for the day

Are you looking for more likes or for more progress?

_____

_____

What is an area you would like to learn more about?

_____

_____

Choose to be great and have a creative positive day!

July 18

"Technology can only take you so far until your social skills come into play"

Questions for the day

Is technology keeping you from great in person conversations?

_____

_____

What are some best practices you use to limit too much daily use of technology?

_____

_____

Choose to be great and have a creative positive day!

July 19

"The transformation you are going through will one day make sense so continue to push forward without looking back"

———

Questions for the day

What are some things in your life that need to be transformed into a positive for your life?

_____

_____

How much time do you allocate on a weekly basis towards personal growth?

_____

_____

Choose to be great and have a creative positive day!

July 20

"Defeat leads to discovery which results in the necessary discipline to win"

Questions for the day

What is the biggest defeat you have ever had?

_____

_____

What discoveries were made that led to getting back on a winning track?

_____

_____

Choose to be great and have a creative positive day!

July 21

*"Attention to detail will lead to organization and structure
necessary to keep a winning advantage"*

———

Questions for the day

How organized is your calendar?

_____

_____

What gets in the way to keep you from a more structured
routine?

_____

_____

Choose to be great and have a creative positive day!

July 22

"Each day is a step towards your greatness make the most of the journey"

Questions for the day

What do you do to celebrate what you feel is progress in your life?

_____

_____

How do you feel about the pace and progress of your goals?

_____

_____

Choose to be great and have a creative positive day!

July 23

"The automation of your life has led to isolation depriving yourself of wisdom"

Questions for the day

Do you feel like you have just scratched the surface of your potential?

_____

_____

How do you focus on self-growth and gain wisdom?

_____

_____

Choose to be great and have a creative positive day!

July 24

"Be creative and create your path even when you do not see one in front of you"

Questions for the day

Are you clear as to the path you are on and are you certain it is the right path?

_____

_____

Do you feel as if you are a creative person?

_____

_____

Choose to be great and have a creative positive day!

July 25

"The only thing that can stunt your growth is your inability to get out of your own way"

———

Questions for the day

How is your mental mind state?

_____

_____

What are some thoughts you need to get out of your mind to enable you to continue your journey?

_____

_____

Choose to be great and have a creative positive day!

July 26

"True confidence will be found when you set aside doubt and conquer your fears"

———

Questions for the day

What is your biggest fear and why?

_____

_____

What are some areas you need to be confident in but lack confidence?

_____

_____

Choose to be great and have a creative positive day!

July 27

"Set aside time to focus on you or one day you will look back with regret and frustration"

Questions for the day

How much time a day do you set aside for your own time?

_____

_____

What are some things you could do starting today to spend more time on just you?

_____

_____

Choose to be great and have a creative positive day!

July 28

*"In theory things may sound good but stop talking
and take action"*

––––––

Questions for the day

What are some things you need to implement but haven't taken
the time to do so?

_____

_____

Do your actions follow your ideas?

_____

_____

Choose to be great and have a creative positive day!

July 29

"Your value will be earned when you have found your character"

Questions for the day

How would you define your character?

_____

_____

How do you determine your value to others?

_____

_____

Choose to be great and have a creative positive day!

July 30

"Stop trying to keep up with others and worry about your own race"

Questions for the day

How do others influence things you think you need?

_____

_____

What more can you do to stay focused on what you truly need to move forward?

_____

_____

Choose to be great and have a creative positive day!

July 31

"Your revival will be the comeback that defines your destiny"

———

Questions for the day

What comeback is needed in your life?

_____

_____

What defines your view of your destiny?

_____

_____

Choose to be great and have a creative positive day!

July 31

August

August 1

"Complacency is the enemy of traction"

———

Questions for the day

Where do you feel stuck?

_____

_____

How do you define pace and progress inside and outside of work?

_____

_____

Choose to be great and have a creative positive day!

August 2

"If your back is up against the wall silence the negativity by removing whatever is in front of you"

Questions for the day

What is the biggest obstacle you are currently facing?

_____

_____

What will it take to remove that obstacle?

_____

_____

Choose to be great and have a creative positive day!

August 3

"The end is near only if you go day to day without hope"

Questions for the day

What truly motivates you?

_____

_____

What does the bigger picture mean for you?

_____

_____

Choose to be great and have a creative positive day!

August 4

"To be a champion you must figure out how to be consistent"

Questions for the day

What one thing do you need to add or takeaway with your daily routine?

_____

_____

Do you feel as if you have consistency in your life?

_____

_____

Choose to be great and have a creative positive day!

QUOTES FOR THE SOUL

August 5

"Judgement is only worth to the one judging only you can put forth the proper perspective of how you want to be viewed"

Questions for the day

How do you feel others perceive you?

_____

_____

How do you want to be viewed?

_____

_____

Choose to be great and have a creative positive day!

August 6

"Truth be told you need a wakeup call more often than you think"

Questions for the day

What is one area that you need to wake up on?

_____

_____

Is there someone around you that you need to give a wakeup call to?

_____

_____

Choose to be great and have a creative positive day!

August 7

"Be careful in the circle you keep as most only want to be in the middle of your circle not just a part of it"

Questions for the day

Do you surround yourself with like-minded individuals?

_____

_____

Do you need to change your surroundings?

_____

_____

Choose to be great and have a creative positive day!

August 8

"Distraction is the key to diversion from your goals and ultimately your progress"

———

Questions for the day

What areas are a distraction in your life currently?

_____

_____

How do you calm the noise?

_____

_____

Choose to be great and have a creative positive day!

August 9

"You cannot simply go straight to the top of the mountain you have to take it step by step and will need some help along the way"

Questions for the day

What mountain are you currently facing?

_____

_____

What help do you need to get to the top?

_____

_____

Choose to be great and have a creative positive day!

August 10

"The journey may be long but the fulfillment will last a lifetime"

———

Questions for the day

How do you feel about your current journey?

_____

_____

How do you know when you are fulfilled?

_____

_____

Choose to be great and have a creative positive day!

August 11

"Your attitude and effort will determine your achievement and excellence"

Questions for the day

Do you have the right attitude to get to where you are trying to go?

_____

_____

How do you define excellence?

_____

_____

Choose to be great and have a creative positive day!

August 12

"Determination will drive your direction so keep your eyes looking forward"

Questions for the day

Do you feel you are on the right path towards your goals?

_____

_____

How do you keep your progress consistent and on the right path?

_____

_____

Choose to be great and have a creative positive day!

August 13

"Fear is only a temporary feeling while peace lasts for an eternity"

Questions for the day

What is a recent fear you had? How did you overcome that fear and move on?

_____

_____

How can you help others overcome fear?

_____

_____

Choose to be great and have a creative positive day!

August 14

"You can be a leader without the title just let your actions show the way"

———

Questions for the day

What can you be doing to go above and beyond?

_____

_____

Is there someone right now you could be influencing?

_____

_____

Choose to be great and have a creative positive day!

August 15

"Greatness can only be defined by your perspective on the level of greatness achieved"

———

Questions for the day

How do you define greatness?

_____

_____

How do you know once you have achieved it?

_____

_____

Choose to be great and have a creative positive day!

August 16

"Everyone must experience turbulence in their life at some point but remember it too shall pass"

Questions for the day

What turbulence are you currently facing in your life?

_____

_____

How do you manage the turbulence you are facing?

_____

_____

Choose to be great and have a creative positive day!

August 17

"Everyone has the same amount of time in their day the difference is the amount of the day you spend executing versus talking about how you will execute"

Questions for the day

Do you have a clear vision and strategy?

_____

_____

What more can you be doing to execute more consistently?

_____

_____

Choose to be great and have a creative positive day!

August 18

"It is easy to say what you want to become but very few actually know how to make what you say a reality"

Questions for the day

What is your ultimate goal?

_____

_____

Are you clear on how to achieve the goal you have set forth?

_____

_____

Choose to be great and have a creative positive day!

August 19

"It is the quality of your work that matters not that quantity of actions behind it"

Questions for the day

Do you feel like you are working smarter not harder?

_____

_____

How can you be more effective with the time you spend working?

_____

_____

Choose to be great and have a creative positive day!

August 20

"In order to prove yourself to the outside world you must be ready to be coached to your inner self"

Questions for the day

What is the biggest area you need coaching in?

_____

_____

Do you feel as if you are vulnerable to candid coaching?

_____

_____

Choose to be great and have a creative positive day!

August 21

"Your true self knows what you need to do in order to push forward so make it happen and keep moving"

Questions for the day

Do you ever feel as if you are being held back?

_____

_____

Are you clear as to why?

_____

_____

Choose to be great and have a creative positive day!

August 22

"Trust can only be earned by giving it away but proceed with caution"

———

Questions for the day

Do you feel as if you have some people around you that you can honestly trust?

_____

_____

How easy is it to earn your trust?

_____

_____

Choose to be great and have a creative positive day!

August 23

"Temptation is only as tempting as the thoughts you spend on being the tempted"

———

Questions for the day

What is a recent temptation you have faced?

_____

_____

How did you overcome that temptation?

_____

_____

Choose to be great and have a creative positive day!

August 24

"We all possess the ability to inspire others so before you can acquire make sure to inspire"

Questions for the day

Who is someone you can go out of your way to inspire today?

_____

_____

Do you feel inspired?

_____

_____

Choose to be great and have a creative positive day!

August 25

"Stop finding reasons you can't and start finding reasons you CAN"

Questions for the day

What can you do to keep a positive environment around you?

_____

_____

What is keeping you from maintaining a positive environment?

_____

_____

Choose to be great and have a creative positive day!

August 26

"You can only be defeated if you have mentally given up"

Questions for the day

When you feel like you wanted to stop what kept you moving forward?

_____

_____

What is a recent story you can share of overcoming defeat?

_____

_____

Choose to be great and have a creative positive day!

QUOTES FOR THE SOUL

August 27

"Victory is in front of you so keep charging forward and do not look back"

Questions for the day

Can you think of a recent victory that you can share to inspire others?

_____

_____

What can you do to lead others to victory around you?

_____

_____

Choose to be great and have a creative positive day!

August 28

"The true test comes when you wake up every day to get out of bed and motivate yourself towards greatness"

Questions for the day

What is your daily motivation?

_____

_____

How disciplined is your daily routine?

_____

_____

Choose to be great and have a creative positive day!

August 29

"Every season shall pass but true growth only occurs if we have learned from the season that just passed"

Questions for the day

What is a recent life lesson you learned?

_____

_____

How can you use that learning to protect others from the same mistakes?

_____

_____

Choose to be great and have a creative positive day!

August 30

"Depression can only linger if the mind is stuck so get out of neutral and get yourself back into gear"

Questions for the day

What are some areas you may have recently felt depressed about?

_____

_____

How did you move past that season in your life?

_____

_____

Choose to be great and have a creative positive day!

August 31

"Triumph comes when consistency meets persistence"

Questions for the day

What was your greatest achievement this month?

_____

_____

What is 1 thing you would have done differently?

_____

_____

Choose to be great and have a creative positive day!

September

September 1

"Inspiration can only come after determination has settled in"

Questions for the day

Do you feel you are truly determined to reach your goals?

_____

_____

How can you keep your determination consistent?

_____

_____

Choose to be great and have a creative positive day!

September 2

"Create the life you want by putting in the work consistently"

Questions for the day

What type of life are you trying to create for yourself?

_____

_____

What more do you need to get there?

_____

_____

Choose to be great and have a creative positive day!

September 3

"Seasons come and go but the moments you create will last a lifetime"

Questions for the day

What is the best vacation you have ever had?

_____

_____

Where is the next place you would like to visit?

_____

_____

Choose to be great and have a creative positive day!

September 4

"In life the choice is yours be great or be average I choose to avoid the second option"

Questions for the day

How do you define greatness?

_____

_____

What can you do today to avoid being average?

_____

_____

Choose to be great and have a creative positive day!

September 5

"Let your hard work and reputation be your introduction to any new person you encounter"

Questions for the day

Do others already have a preconceived notion of who you are?

_____

_____

What can you do to maintain a positive image?

_____

_____

Choose to be great and have a creative positive day!

September 6

"Do not let anyone stand in your way of progress it is up to you to move forward without distraction"

Questions for the day

Do those around you have your best interest?

_____

_____

What can you do to expedite the achievement of your goals?

_____

_____

Choose to be great and have a creative positive day!

September 7

"Yesterday has nothing left for you, today is waiting, and tomorrow is a timeless thought"

Questions for the day

Do you really feel that today has all of your attention?

_____

_____

What do you do to stay focused on the moment?

_____

_____

Choose to be great and have a creative positive day!

September 8

"Every now and then we find a jewel of an idea so make sure you are seeking and not wondering through life"

Questions for the day

What is a recent idea you came up with to make an impact towards your goals?

_____

_____

Do you seek out knowledge or rely on the acumen of others around you?

_____

_____

Choose to be great and have a creative positive day!

September 9

"Sense of urgency is needed in order to execute in a timely manner"

———

Questions for the day

How do you handle those around you that you feel do not share the same work ethic as you?

_____

_____

What do you do if you are struggling with responsiveness from your peers and leaders you may work with?

_____

_____

Choose to be great and have a creative positive day!

September 10

"To define your self-worth is to first be vulnerable to address your weaknesses"

———

Questions for the day

How do you define self-worth?

_____

_____

Are you clear on where your weaknesses are and how to address them?

_____

_____

Choose to be great and have a creative positive day!

September 11

"Positivity is the enemy of negativity so create the environment you want to dwell in now"

Questions for the day

How is your personal and professional environment?

_____

_____

Does anything need to change in order to maintain a positive environment?

_____

_____

Choose to be great and have a creative positive day!

September 12

"If you have a passion and purpose for what you do you will never truly work your entire life"

———

Questions for the day

What do you feel is your purpose in life?

_____

_____

Do you feel you are serving your purpose?

_____

_____

Choose to be great and have a creative positive day!

September 13

"Perhaps the greatest tool you can be equipped with is character so ensure yours is in order"

———

Questions for the day

What is the most important character lesson you have learned?

_____

_____

What are some things you do to maintain a good character?

_____

_____

Choose to be great and have a creative positive day!

September 14

*"Learning how to fail only prepares the way
for ultimate victory"*

Questions for the day

What do you feel is your biggest failure?

_____

_____

What is your biggest victory?

_____

_____

Choose to be great and have a creative positive day!

September 15

"The journey to the top may seem long but the feeling of achievement will last forever"

Questions for the day

How do you maintain endurance towards your goals?

_____

_____

What is the greatest achievement you have ever had?

_____

_____

Choose to be great and have a creative positive day!

September 16

"Beware of those around you looking for handouts as often you are the one left empty-handed"

———

Questions for the day

Do you give more than you receive?

_____

_____

When you do give is it just from a monetary perspective or something else?

_____

_____

Choose to be great and have a creative positive day!

September 17

"Destroy your fears by consuming fellowship"

Questions for the day

Where do you go to find fellowship?

_____

_____

What steps can you take to continually overcome any fears you may have?

_____

_____

Choose to be great and have a creative positive day!

September 18

"Sometimes it is the little things that add up to make the biggest moment arrive"

Questions for the day

What is something you are currently waiting on?

_____

_____

What are some of the key steps you have taken in life to get you where you are today?

_____

_____

Choose to be great and have a creative positive day!

September 19

"Trust has to be given away to receive it back so stop holding on"

—————

Questions for the day

Share a time it was hard for you to trust someone and it worked out in your favor?

———————————————————

———————————————————

 Is there someone today you need to start trusting more in your life?

———————————————————

———————————————————

Choose to be great and have a creative positive day!

September 20

You were meant for something great do not doubt what is inside you and charge forward"

Questions for the day

What is one thing you can do each morning to start your day on a positive note?

_____

_____

What are some doubts you are currently faced with?

_____

_____

Choose to be great and have a creative positive day!

September 21

"If you fall down have confidence you can form a support system to lift you back up and get you back on track"

———

Questions for the day

Who do you share your goals with?

_____

_____

Do you feel you have a safety net if failure occurs and you need to get back on track?

_____

_____

Choose to be great and have a creative positive day!

September 22

"Your engagement can be contagious so make sure to spread it as fast as you can to those around you"

Questions for the day

What are some things you do to engage those around you?

_____

_____

Do you feel as if you are operating in an engaged environment?

_____

_____

Choose to be great and have a creative positive day!

September 23

"Conflict may arise but it is up to you to write the next line in your story"

Questions for the day

How do you handle adversity?

_____

_____

What is a current conflict you may be facing?

_____

_____

Choose to be great and have a creative positive day!

September 24

"Perseverance is your way of not giving up and ensuring completion of the task at hand"

Questions for the day

What is a current task you are struggling with completing?

_____

_____

What do you do to persevere when times get tough?

_____

_____

Choose to be great and have a creative positive day!

September 25

"The energy it takes for you to think negative thoughts is wasted and better spent on positive momentum"

———

Questions for the day

What are some brain exercises you can do to ensure a positive mental state?

_____

_____

How do you keep pushing forward when faced with a negative situation?

_____

_____

Choose to be great and have a creative positive day!

September 26

"Make your life matter do not think you are not loud enough to be heard"

———

Questions for the day

What are some things in your community you could be doing to serve others?

_____

_____

How can you make sure your voice is heard as a voice of influence?

_____

_____

Choose to be great and have a creative positive day!

September 27

"Influence is a powerful tool use it wisely to impact others"

Questions for the day

What do you do to influence those around you?

_____

_____

Who has the most influence on you?

_____

_____

Choose to be great and have a creative positive day!

September 28

"Today you can chose to be great or just let another opportunity go unopened"

———

Questions for the day

What do you feel is your next opportunity in front of you?

_____

_____

How do you prevent procrastination and push forward?

_____

_____

Choose to be great and have a creative positive day!

September 29

"All of the Sundays of my youth meant something to me so keep your eyes on the big picture"

Questions for the day

What role does faith play in your life?

_____

_____

What is your big picture?

_____

_____

Choose to be great and have a creative positive day!

September 30

"If you have already thought about defeat then consider yourself defeated"

Questions for the day

How do you overcome thinking you cannot do something?

_____

_____

What can you do to help those around you push forward?

_____

_____

Choose to be great and have a creative positive day!

October

October

October 1

"Loyalty is a word often not appreciated anymore so make sure it is rewarded"

———

Questions for the day

Where has loyalty brought you in your current life?

_____

_____

How do you reward those who are loyal around you?

_____

_____

Choose to be great and have a creative positive day!

October 2

"Do not be fooled when something is too good to be true make sure to read through the lines"

———

Questions for the day

Share a time you felt something was too good to be true?

_____

_____

How do you quickly identify what may be fake around you?

_____

_____

Choose to be great and have a creative positive day!

October 3

"Regret is quickly overcome by fulfillment"

Questions for the day

What is your biggest regret in life?

_____

_____

What fulfillment in your life has helped to overcome your regrets?

_____

_____

Choose to be great and have a creative positive day!

October 4

"Any storm is temporary remember sunshine is always behind the dark clouds"

———

Questions for the day

What is a current storm you may be faced with?

_____

_____

What are some things you do to put the storm behind you and head into the sunshine?

_____

_____

Choose to be great and have a creative positive day!

October 5

"The best bet you can ever make is on the abilities you have to find success so why not double down all day long"

Questions for the day

What is the biggest gamble you ever took in your life?

_____

_____

What was the result?

_____

_____

Choose to be great and have a creative positive day!

October 6

"Yesterday cannot help you, today is waiting to be conquered, and tomorrow is not a reality"

———

Questions for the day

What is something you need to conquer today?

_____

_____

How do you stay in the moment and not let your mind drift?

_____

_____

Choose to be great and have a creative positive day!

October 7

*"Just because you have reached your destination does not
mean your journey is over in fact it has just begun"*

———

Questions for the day

What do you do to celebrate your achievement of a goal?

_____

_____

How do you ensure to not just settle for where you are?

_____

_____

Choose to be great and have a creative positive day!

October 8

"Striving for greatness can only occur if the proper mental stretching has taken place"

Questions for the day

How do you feel about your current mental state?

_____

_____

What can you do to make sure traction is taking place and you are not stuck where you are?

_____

_____

Choose to be great and have a creative positive day!

October 9

"Become the type of person you know you can be by outwardly defining who you are"

Questions for the day

What do you feel is your self-image to others?

_____

_____

Does your self-image portray the true person you are?

_____

_____

Choose to be great and have a creative positive day!

October 10

"Consistency in your behaviors will lead to consistency in your
results one is empty without the other"

———

Questions for the day

What are some of the behaviors you attribute your success to?

_____

_____

What are some things you do in order to ensure consistency in your behaviors to drive results?

_____

_____

Choose to be great and have a creative positive day!

October 11

"Skills are important but your competencies can allow you to thrive if only given the right opportunity"

———

Questions for the day

What are some of your strongest competencies?

_____

_____

What are some competencies you would like to further develop?

_____

_____

Choose to be great and have a creative positive day!

October 12

"Action speaks louder than words so stop talking and focus
on
making things happen"

Questions for the day

What are some actions you need to take today to make progress with a task you are currently facing?

_____

_____

What do you do to make things happen instead of let things happen around you?

_____

_____

Choose to be great and have a creative positive day!

October 13

"Stop looking at what you do not have and start looking at what matters"

———

Questions for the day

Do you feel as if you are always comparing yourself to others?

_____

_____

What are some things you do to focus on what truly matters in your life?

_____

_____

Choose to be great and have a creative positive day!

October 14

"Discipline is the enemy of laziness so get up and go"

Questions for the day

What are some things you do to avoid procrastination?

_____

_____

What are some disciplines you need in your life in order to drive more consistent results?

_____

_____

Choose to be great and have a creative positive day!

October 15

"Stop waiting and start creating which is fueled by changing your current circumstance"

Questions for the day

What are some things you have been wanting to create?

_____

_____

How can you change the circumstance around you to be more productive?

_____

_____

Choose to be great and have a creative positive day!

October 16

"Perhaps your discovery stage in your life will be your greatest awakening"

Questions for the day

When you search your soul what do you find?

_____

_____

What awakening is needed in your life?

_____

_____

Choose to be great and have a creative positive day!

October 17

"True growth cannot occur unless you have learned from the past not just dealt with it"

―――――

Questions for the day

Share a time where you felt true growth occurred?

_____

_____

How have you moved on from some not so great memories of the past?

_____

_____

Choose to be great and have a creative positive day!

October 18

"To shed a tear to grow past fear means success must be near"

———

Questions for the day

Share the last time you had a good cry and why?

_____

_____

How did you use that lesson to move forward and ultimately on to achievement?

_____

_____

Choose to be great and have a creative positive day!

October 19

"To second guess is to say the first guess did not have much thought behind it so stop your self-doubt and press forward"

———

Questions for the day

What do you do to create time to relax and just think through your thoughts?

_____

_____

How can you eliminate self-doubt?

_____

_____

Choose to be great and have a creative positive day!

October 20

"Do not be the one that years from now you find yourself stuck in the world of I wish"

———

Questions for the day

What is keeping you from making progress on your goals?

_____

_____

How do you avoid regrets in your life?

_____

_____

Choose to be great and have a creative positive day!

October 21

"Pace and Progress and will lead to Poise and Process"

———

Questions for the day

How does pace and progress show up in your life?

_____

_____

Do you have a defined process that will lead to success?

_____

_____

Choose to be great and have a creative positive day!

October 22

"You are only limited by the person looking back at you every morning in the mirror so let that person know you chose to be great"

———

Questions for the day

What are some things you do to start your day?

_____

_____

What do you see when you look in your mirror?

_____

_____

Choose to be great and have a creative positive day!

October 23

"You have 86,400 reasons to create the positive environment around you necessary to win so do not waste a second"

———

Questions for the day

How much time do you feel you waste each day on negativity?

_____

_____

Does your body and verbal language reflect your true character?

_____

_____

Choose to be great and have a creative positive day!

October 24

"There are plenty of managers and never enough true leaders so choose to lead from the front and leave the titles at the door"

———

Questions for the day

Who are some of the great leaders that have influenced you?

_____

_____

How can you be a leader even if you do not have the title?

_____

_____

Choose to be great and have a creative positive day!

October 25

"Change the game do not just be a player stuck in the game"

Questions for the day

Who are some of the great leaders that have influenced you?

_____

_____

What steps can you take to avoid just going through the motions?

_____

_____

Choose to be great and have a creative positive day!

October 26

"Let go and open your mind to consume from others as you certainly do not have all of the answers"

Questions for the day

What are some things you need to let go of in your life?

_____

_____

What can you be doing to learn more from others?

_____

_____

Choose to be great and have a creative positive day!

October 27

"The race can only be won if the proper pace has been maintained all the way through"

———

Questions for the day

What do you do to stay on track?

_____

_____

When you feel like giving up what keeps you going?

_____

_____

Choose to be great and have a creative positive day!

October 28

"Mental fitness is arguably more important than physical fitness so make sure proper training is in place to reach your destination"

———

Questions for the day

What routines do you have in place for mental/physical fitness?

_____

_____

What gets in the way of making progress in these areas?

_____

_____

Choose to be great and have a creative positive day!

October 29

"When others doubt your capabilities use their doubt as your fuel for action"

Questions for the day

Share a recent time someone doubted you and you proved them wrong?

_____

_____

How do you use negativity to drive positive reaction?

_____

_____

Choose to be great and have a creative positive day!

October 30

"Practice makes progress do not worry about perfection"

Questions for the day

What are some areas you need more practice in?

_____

_____

What benchmarks do you use to ensure progress is being made?

_____

_____

Choose to be great and have a creative positive day!

October 31

"Do not be scared about anything instead use your positive thoughts to drive out fear"

Questions for the day

What has you currently in a state of fear?

_____

_____

What are some things you can do to make sure you are not scared of what may be next and that you stay positive?

_____

_____

Choose to be great and have a creative positive day!

November

November 1

"The ultimate goal for you should be that your life mattered and you made an impact"

———

Questions for the day

How do you feel about the impact you are making to those around you?

_____

_____

What more can you be doing to give back to the community around you?

_____

_____

Choose to be great and have a creative positive day!

November 2

"While others try to solve their identity crisis you can rise above and define your true self"

Questions for the day

What is your identity?

_____

_____

How do you stay true to who you are?

_____

_____

Choose to be great and have a creative positive day!

November 3

"Wishful thinking leads to wasteful draining so choose your thoughts wisely"

Questions for the day

What are some thoughts going through your mind right now as you comment on today's quote?

_____

_____

How can you avoid a world of what if?

_____

_____

Choose to be great and have a creative positive day!

November 4

"You will only go as far as you mental determination will take you so keep your mental state in high gear"

Questions for the day

How to you maintain a positive outlook on your life?

_____

_____

What do you need to do in order to pick up the pace towards your goals?

_____

_____

Choose to be great and have a creative positive day!

November 5

"A breakthrough is trying to take place so stop resisting and start to embrace"

Questions for the day

What breakthrough is needed in your life?

_____

_____

What is holding you back from embracing change?

_____

_____

Choose to be great and have a creative positive day!

November 6

"Courage is needed to drive out fear of the unknown which serves as an obstacle to your success"

Questions for the day

What obstacles are you currently facing?

_____

_____

How do you overcome fear of the unknown?

_____

_____

Choose to be great and have a creative positive day!

November 7

"Let your logo be the impression you leave behind each person you meet"

Questions for the day

If you had to design a logo of yourself what symbol would represent you?

_____

_____

What type of impression do you want to leave others with about you?

_____

_____

Choose to be great and have a creative positive day!

November 8

*"Be your own champion that others can look up to stop looking
for a hero"*

Questions for the day

How can you separate yourself from your competition?

_____

_____

What is holding you back from being viewed as a hero/mentor to someone else?

_____

_____

Choose to be great and have a creative positive day!

November 9

"Your personality will drive more business than your intelligence"

———

Questions for the day

How good do you feel about your social skills?

_____

_____

How can you grow more in your interpersonal skills to be more outwardly effective?

_____

_____

Choose to be great and have a creative positive day!

November 10

"Your belief of who you are will be the baseline from where all future growth occurs"

———

Questions for the day

Share a time that you truly believed in yourself to reach a specific milestone in your life?

_____

_____

What lessons learned can help others along their journey?

_____

_____

Choose to be great and have a creative positive day!

November 11

"Get out of your head, out of your bed, and motivate"

Questions for the day

Name 1 thing you want to accomplish today?

_____

_____

What obstacles are in your way and how do you plan on over-coming them?

_____

_____

Choose to be great and have a creative positive day!

November 12

"In order to captivate your audience you must first establish who your audience is"

Questions for the day

Who do you consider to be your fans?

_____

_____

Are you clear on who you are trying to target to be in your circle?

_____

_____

Choose to be great and have a creative positive day!

November 13

"The pressure you create for yourself could be better served towards the behaviors you need to be executing towards success"

Questions for the day

Share a recent situation where you were under pressure and had to perform?

_____

_____

What was the result and what did you learn from that situation?

_____

_____

Choose to be great and have a creative positive day!

November 14

"Start today with enthusiasm and create the energy you want others to feed off of to make it a great day"

Questions for the day

What can you be doing to motivate others around you?

_____

_____

How can you build positive energy for those around you to start their day?

_____

_____

Choose to be great and have a creative positive day!

November 15

"Dare to be great not average for you were created to do so much more"

Questions for the day

Name 1 thing you can do today to be great?

_____

_____

What is the long term impact if you choose to blend in and not truly discover your self-worth?

_____

_____

Choose to be great and have a creative positive day!

November 16

"Praises will come, raises will come but satisfaction is yours to define"

Questions for the day

When is the last time you felt true satisfaction?

_____

_____

When do you know if you are satisfied with your results?

_____

_____

Choose to be great and have a creative positive day!

November 17

"Humility drives ability leading to stability"

Questions for the day

Do others see you as humble or over the top?

_____

_____

How can you use humility to inspire others around you?

_____

_____

Choose to be great and have a creative positive day!

November 18

"I am only as good as my last accomplishment wrong I am only as good as my thinking allows"

Questions for the day

Share a time where your disbelief limited your progress?

_____

_____

What gets in your way of positive thinking?

_____

_____

Choose to be great and have a creative positive day!

November 19

"Do not choose when to go hard or ease up rather maintain a good speed and charge forward"

Questions for the day

How do you feel about your current work ethic?

_____

_____

Anything you would change?

_____

_____

Choose to be great and have a creative positive day!

November 20

"You are the CEO of you so do not let anyone think they can rule over you"

Questions for the day

Do you feel like you are under someone's shadow?

_____

_____

What are some things you can do today to take charge of your life?

_____

_____

Choose to be great and have a creative positive day!

November 21

"Do not let the day run you rather you own your own day and drive the necessary outcomes you need to deliver on to push forward"

Questions for the day

How organized is your calendar?

_____

_____

Do you set aside planning time for your personal development?

_____

_____

Choose to be great and have a creative positive day!

November 22

"Dominate at every level until your work speaks for itself"

Questions for the day

What are some areas you know you need to dominate in to reach the next level of your journey?

_____

_____

Do you have the tools and resources you need to get to where you are going?

_____

_____

Choose to be great and have a creative positive day!

November 23

"The levels of success are only defined by your perception of what those levels really are"

Questions for the day

What does success look like to you?

_____

_____

What is the next level of success you are looking to reach?

_____

_____

Choose to be great and have a creative positive day!

November 24

"Rather than always asking what do you do for a living why not spin it to while you are living what are you going to do to impact those around you"

Questions for the day

As the holidays approach what can you do to impact your community or someone in need?

_____

_____

How can you get others in action around you to do the same?

_____

_____

Choose to be great and have a creative positive day!

November 25

"I am not defined by wins and loses I am defined by living my passion and purpose"

Questions for the day

What is your true passion?

_____

_____

Do you feel like you have a chance to live your passion throughout your journey?

_____

_____

Choose to be great and have a creative positive day!

November 26

"To acquire is to achieve temporary happiness to inspire is to achieve lasting legacy"

———

Questions for the day

How do you separate the need for material acquisition versus inspiring others around you?

_____

_____

What is the legacy you want to leave behind?

_____

_____

Choose to be great and have a creative positive day!

November 27

"Give me a pen and paper and I will give you a future and a plan"

Questions for the day

Do you feel clear on the plan for your future?

_____

_____

What is your roadmap to get there?

_____

_____

Choose to be great and have a creative positive day!

November 28

"True leadership occurs when a fire is lit inside someone not just under them"

———

Questions for the day

What does it take for someone to inspire you to do more than you are used to doing?

_____

_____

Who is someone that needs a fire lit inside of them starting today?

_____

_____

Choose to be great and have a creative positive day!

November 29

"Visualize the success you are working towards so that when times get tough you can see through the storm to the victory waiting on the other side"

———

Questions for the day

How do you visualize your goals?

_____

_____

What tools do you use to ensure you do not take your eye off the ball?

_____

_____

Choose to be great and have a creative positive day!

November 30

"In order to get better you must first acknowledge your opportunities for improvement"

Questions for the day

What tools do you use to identify your opportunities for improvement?

_____

_____

How often do you assess your progress?

_____

_____

Choose to be great and have a creative positive day!

December

December

December 1

"The last month of the year should serve as a reminder to finish out the tasks set forth to start the year"

Questions for the day

Coming into the last month of the year how are you feeling about what you set out to accomplish this year?

_____

_____

Anything you would have done differently up to now?

_____

_____

Choose to be great and have a creative positive day!

December 2

"To be self-serving is a disservice to all of those who believe in your ability to influence others"

———

Questions for the day

How do you handle self-serving people that may be around you?

_____

_____

How do you prevent from appearing self-serving to others?

_____

_____

Choose to be great and have a creative positive day!

December 3

Progress is the enemy of procrastination so get out of your own way and fight the good fight"

———

Questions for the day

How do you feel about your progress and growth this year?

_____

_____

If it has not been what you thought it would be what can you start doing today to change your course of direction?

_____

_____

Choose to be great and have a creative positive day!

December 4

"You cannot discover what is waiting for you if you do not open your eyes wide open to the endless possibilities that await"

Questions for the day

Share one thing you have discovered about yourself this year?

_____

_____

What can you do for others around you to help them discover their potential?

_____

_____

Choose to be great and have a creative positive day!

December 5

"Ambition should be your ammunition for fruition in your life"

———

Questions for the day

What are some of your current ambitions?

_____

_____

What can you do to take more time to learn about others ambitions around you?

_____

_____

Choose to be great and have a creative positive day!

December 6

"Time is not going to wait for you to live out your destiny so seize the moment and own the day"

———

Questions for the day

What is 1 thing you must get done today?

_____

_____

What can you do today to impact your progress on your goals?

_____

_____

Choose to be great and have a creative positive day!

December 7

"Social Media could be distracting you from progress so sign out and sign in to your growth plan"

———

Questions for the day

How much of your day is spent on social media if you had to guess?

_____

_____

How much of your day is spent on working towards your goals?

_____

_____

Choose to be great and have a creative positive day!

December 8

"It is not the intensity towards your goals it is the propensity of the milestones you can reach if you believe in yourself"

Questions for the day

Are you approaching your goals with intensity or consistency?

_____

_____

Do you set stretch goals for yourself?

_____

_____

Choose to be great and have a creative positive day!

December 9

"Sleep is important to awaken to a mental state of winning"

Questions for the day

How much sleep on average do you get?

_____

_____

Do you have any routines you do before bed in order to ensure a good night's rest?

_____

_____

Choose to be great and have a creative positive day!

December 10

*"The journey is long but the joy from achievement cannot have
the length of time placed on it"*

———

Questions for the day

When is the last time you experienced true joy?

_____

_____

What were some obstacles you had to overcome to achieve that joy in
your life?

_____

_____

Choose to be great and have a creative positive day!

December 11

"To self-reflect is to self-select versus self-deflect your ability to achieve"

Questions for the day

How much time do you take to reflect on your progress?

_____

_____

When is the last time you truly assessed where you are at in life versus where you want to be?

_____

_____

Choose to be great and have a creative positive day!

December 12

"Make the impossible possible by removing mountains with your attitude and effort towards each day"

Questions for the day

What are some mountains you need moved out of your way today?

_____

_____

_____

Share a recent time where you felt something was impossible and you made it possible.

_____

_____

_____

Choose to be great and have a creative positive day!

December 13

"A manager manages to their own agenda a leader lets their people define who they are"

―――――

Questions for the day

Who is the greatest leader you have ever worked for?

_____

_____

What are some traits they had that made them great in your eyes?

_____

_____

Choose to be great and have a creative positive day!

December 14

"To follow is to conform while to lead is to differentiate"

———

Questions for the day

Do you view yourself as a follower or a leader?

_____

_____

What can you do to differentiate yourself from others?

_____

_____

Choose to be great and have a creative positive day!

December 15

"The feeling of exhaustion can never match the feeling of accomplishment"

Questions for the day

What do you do when feeling exhausted in your daily routines to push forward?

_____

_____

What tools can you share with the group to ensure no one hits the burn out stage?

_____

_____

Choose to be great and have a creative positive day!

December 16

"You are the author of your own story only you can determine if it is worth reading"

Questions for the day

If you had to write a book about you what would be the title?

_____

_____

What would you want your readers to take away from reading the book?

_____

_____

Choose to be great and have a creative positive day!

December 17

"The pain you may feel along your journey will be temporary compared to the lasting feeling of success once you have crossed the finish line"

Questions for the day

Share with the group one of the most painful moments in your life?

_____

_____

How did you get through that pain and what ultimately led you to success?

_____

_____

Choose to be great and have a creative positive day!

December 18

*"Communication is key in getting the desired outcomes
you are seeking"*

———

Questions for the day

Are you clear in your expectations you have of others?

_____

_____

What are some things you can be doing better to communicate?

_____

_____

Choose to be great and have a creative positive day!

December 19

"Experience is only as good as the growth that came from it"

Questions for the day

What is a recent personal growth experience that has happened for you?

_____

_____

What lesson did you learn from that experience?

_____

_____

Choose to be great and have a creative positive day!

December 20

"Knowledge of self and knowledge of others can prevent adversity when forming a partnership"

Questions for the day

What things do you do in order to truly get to know someone?

_____

_____

Do you understand the different personalities around you and what it takes to have a relationship with each person?

_____

_____

Choose to be great and have a creative positive day!

December 21

"Raise your level of intensity to match the pace needed to reach your destiny"

Questions for the day

How high do you set your goals?

_____

_____

Are you moving at the speed necessary to reach your destiny?

_____

_____

Choose to be great and have a creative positive day!

December 22

"Your daily to do list should reflect actionable items necessary for growth"

Questions for the day

What is on your to do list today?

_____

_____

Do those items reflect things that will enable growth?

_____

_____

Choose to be great and have a creative positive day!

December 23

"Your appetite for success needs to be big enough to swallow your pride and achieve greatness"

Questions for the day

What are some things you can be doing to ensure you are not prideful and are making progress towards your goals?

_____

_____

What can you do to coach those around you to avoid being prideful?

_____

_____

Choose to be great and have a creative positive day!

December 24

"Keep your aim high and do not settle falling short of your target"

Questions for the day

Are you goals high enough to stretch you past your limits?

_____

_____

How do you stop yourself from falling short of your goals?

_____

_____

Choose to be great and have a creative positive day!

December 25

"Let today serve as a rebirth of the person you know you can be"

———————

Questions for the day

What does a rebirth mean to you?

_____

_____

What can you do today to spread some holiday cheer to someone in need around you?

_____

_____

Choose to be great and have a creative positive day!

December 26

*"The distance from good to great can be measured by the
length of time it takes for you to realize your own value"*

———

Questions for the day

Share a recent time where you added value to a situation you
were in.

_____

_____

What are some tools you use to add value to others in a meaningful way?

_____

_____

Choose to be great and have a creative positive day!

December 27

"Social Selling is here now so get out from behind the curtain and grow your brand"

Questions for the day

What are some tools you use to grow your brand?

_____

_____

What does social selling mean to you?

_____

_____

Choose to be great and have a creative positive day!

December 28

"Your thoughtfulness will shine through any situation if you are genuine in your approach"

Questions for the day

What is a recent situation where your genuine nature made a difference?

_____

_____

Who is someone that could use your genuine nature today?

_____

_____

Choose to be great and have a creative positive day!

December 29

"You do not need to own the whole pie just make sure to carve out your piece"

Questions for the day

As the year comes to an end do you feel good about what you have accomplished this past year?

_____

_____

How do you feel about your personal growth?

_____

_____

Choose to be great and have a creative positive day!

December 30

"When facing a crossroad choose the path that will produce the greatest return on your effort"

Questions for the day

What is a current tough decision you are facing?

_____

_____

What is the expected outcome if you make the wrong decision?

_____

_____

Choose to be great and have a creative positive day!

December 31

"As one year ends and another year enters do not get lost in the noise instead rise above and create the sound of positivity necessary to reach your greatness"

———

Questions for the day

What was your biggest accomplishment this year?

_____

_____

What was your biggest regret?

_____

_____

Choose to be great and have a creative positive day!

www.ingramcontent.com/pod-product-compliance
Lightning Source LLC
Chambersburg PA
CBHW061559110426
42742CB00038B/1553